All rights reserved. No part of this book may be reproduced or transmitted in any form or by any means, electrical or mechanical, including photo copying, recording or by any information storage and retrieval system, without the written consent of the publisher.

Published by Richard J. Soltys Productions
P.O. Box 1501
La Quinta, CA 92253 USA
e-mail: rjsoltys@easyfeed.com
Please contact us at www.rjsp.com for further information.

Printing by USAsia Press, Folsom, California 95630
Dave Ingland, Executive Director
Orlando Ramos, Graphic Designer
Pamela Muscarella, Printing Coordinator
Mike Makkouk, Photographic Coordinator
Michael Smith, Assistant Editor
Second Printing - 2005
Printed in South Korea

Coachella Valley Yesterday, Today and Tomorrow
ISBN 0-9726856-0-x
Copyright MMIII Richard J. Soltys Productions, La Quinta, CA

Coachella Valley
Yesterday, Today and Tomorrow

IV

Grove of Washingtonia filifera fan palms in Indian Canyon - Palm Springs

Coachella Valley
Yesterday, Today and Tomorrow

By Richard J. Soltys

VI

Old schoolhouse on the Torres Martinez Indian Reservation near the Salton Sea

*To the people
of Coachella Valley
with appreciation
for the world they created.*

VIII

Palm Desert - Circa 1950

Coachella Valley
Yesterday, Today and Tomorrow

Coachella Valley Yesterday, Today and Tomorrow is a photographic journey of the Coachella Valley from the beginning when Native Americans first started to populate this desert.

Through stunning black and white historical photographs and new color photography, Richard J. Soltys captures the visual progression of the Coachella Valley from when the valley was nothing more than an immense, barren wasteland. The remarkable historical photographs, coupled with exciting new visuals of the valley today, are in themselves a natural historical narrative of the Coachella Valley.

Richard J. Soltys' relationship to the Coachella Valley extends back to the mid-eighties when he became involved in producing film and video documentaries for local clients, mostly in the water and agriculture areas. Uncovering historical photographs from local collections for use in his productions, he has assembled this pictorial perspective for Coachella Valley Yesterday, Today and Tomorrow. Richard J. Soltys is a writer, producer and director of documentaries for numerous corporate clients. He resides in La Quinta, California with his wife.

Incredible bird life at the Salton Sea.

ACKNOWLEDGEMENTS

Many people helped make this book a reality and I thank them all
for their contributions, large and small.

I am particular grateful to Dennis Mahr and Kathy Papan
of the Coachella Valley Water District,
the Palm Springs Historical Society,
Coachella Valley Historical Society and Museum,
Imperial Irrigation District, General Patton Museum,
Dan Callahan of the Historical Society of Palm Desert,
City of Indian Wells, City of Rancho Mirage,
Cathedral City Historical Society, Joshua Tree National Park,
Racquet Club Hotel & Spa, Palm Springs,
Riverside County Fair & National Date Festival,
City of Coachella and Coachella Chamber of Commerce,
the Anza-Borrego Desert Natural History Association,
Two Bunch Palms, Sidewinder Grill, Cabot Yerxa Museum, Desert Hot Springs
and the Desert Water Agency, Palm Springs.

Brilliant spring bloom in the Santa Rosa Mountains near Palm Desert

This book is dedicated

to Mary Frances, wife and friend,

and to the many associates

who contributed to the creation

of this book.

XIV

Wind farm electric generators and main rail line at the base of Mt. San Jacinto

Contents

Chapter		Page
I	Introduction	19
II	In the Beginning	25
III	Modern Exploration	33
IV	The Coming of the Railroads	39
V	The People Come	43
VI	City of Palm Springs	47
VII	America's First Freeway	53
VIII	City of Indio	59
IX	City of Coachella	67
X	The Date Industry	75
XI	The Salton Sea	85
XII	Coachella Valley Goes to War	93
XIII	The Movie Colony	99
XIV	Coachella Valley Water	105
XV	City of Desert Hot Springs	115
XVI	Joshua Tree National Park	123
XVII	City of Indian Wells	131
XVIII	City of Palm Desert	143
XIX	City of Rancho Mirage	157
XX	City of Cathedral City	165
XXI	City of La Quinta	173
XXII	Coachella Valley's Future	185

XVI

Historic aerial view of Palm Springs in the 1930s

Foreword

It is often said that that there are two Coachella Valleys - one visited by tourists and the one known to those who make the Coachella Valley their home. For the visitor, the Coachella Valley is often golf, tennis, swimming, restaurants, star gazing on balmy nights or just relaxing in the warm sun. Every year millions of visitors come to the Coachella Valley to escape from the colder climes of the Midwest and East or from the drenching rains of the Pacific Northwest. For many of these visitors, reared in a world of seasons or crowded cities, the Coachella Valley is a haven, a paradise.

For the resident, the physical beauty of the Coachella Valley is just part of the appeal, for beyond the uniqueness of desert life is the spirit engendered by those who live here. It doesn't happen overnight by new arrivals but it does happen. Old timers call it "the sand in your shoes syndrome." The Coachella Valley slowly but surely turns visitors into diehard believers of the desert lifestyle. It is not a quality that is easy to express in a few words. It's more a "spirit" that invades the mindset. It's the clean air, the deep blue sky, it's being touched by the hand of nature, and yes, it's the golf, tennis, swimming, the balmy evenings and the warm sun. It's a gentleness in the approach to life. The Coachella Valley is more than a seventy-five mile long and twenty mile wide valley surrounded on three sides by towering mountains. It's a mix of three cultures - Anglo, Hispanic and Indian - a blending of cultures for the betterment of all. And yet, the recent Coachella Valley history since the discovery of water extends back just a little more than a hundred years.

Upon my arrival in the Coachella Valley as a resident six years ago, I was as uninformed of this history and culture as are most new residents. Given an assignment to produce a video documentary to interpret the history of the Coachella Valley opened my eyes to the things that have had impact in the development of Coachella Valley - the dynamic agriculture industry, tourism, the development of water resources, the Salton Sea and the building of the infrastructure by the municipalities to carry the Coachella Valley far into the future. As compared to other regions of the country, these issues are all relatively new and they opened my eyes to telling this pictorial story, Coachella Valley Yesterday, Today and Tomorrow, to bring an appreciation of the transformation that has taken place here during the past years. I believe that the Coachella Valley is now poised to advance into an enterprising future, a future without bounds.

I came to the Coachella Valley with a great deal of naiveté about the valley, sharing the limited perception about the valley common to many new arrivals. It is my hope that this book will impart to the visitor, residents and new arrivals an intuitive glimmer of the transition that permitted a seemingly worthless, barren desert to evolve into one of the most dynamic locations in which to live or visit.

Welcome to the Coachella Valley.
Richard J. Soltys

Introduction

Introduction

In the beginning, the Coachella Valley lay beneath the waters of the north end of the Gulf of California. Billions of years ago, catastrophic changes were taking place on the North American continent, resulting in the upheaval of the Rocky Mountains. As the land rose and climactic transformation took place, winter weather covered the mountains deep with snow. The runoff from the snowmelt fathered one of the world's great rivers, the mighty Colorado. With origins high in the Rocky Mountains, the river raced across the continent on its rush to reach the sea. The waters ripped away at the land creating the massive Grand Canyon, one of the most incredible geologic transformations in the world.

For billions of years the flowing water carried rock, silt and soil down some 1,400 miles to be deposited into the Gulf of California. As the soil built up at the end of the river, it parted the Gulf, creating an ancient inland sea that covered the southern most extremes of California. Beneath the waters, the sea bottom would eventually become known as the Coachella Valley.

As the waters evaporated, the barren landscape became a part of the vast expanse of desert that covered the Southwestern part of the United States. For untold time the land lay exposed, at the mercy of the elements. Ripped and torn by desert winds, a river trying to fulfill its destiny, the land was eroded by infrequent torrential storms. Eon after eon, the land slumbered under the blazing sun - a vast expanse of seemingly worthless, isolated terrain. That was long, long ago. In the late 1800s, man discovered the geologic formation that brought life to Coachella Valley, an underground aquifer beneath the desert floor.

For little more than a century, the Coachella Valley evolved into one of the world's great communities. Driven by agriculture, the valley has become a fertile and productive farming area growing crops twelve months out of the year. The combination of water, sun and soil allowed the Coachella Valley to grow into America's citrus, grape, vegetable and salad bowl, helping to feed America and the world.

As the Coachella Valley became established, the people came, at first on foot, horse, wagon and train - and with today's modern transportation systems, by car and jet airplane. People from every part of the world are discovering this valley, be they presidents, royalty, scientists, heads of state, the famous and the not so famous. Most come here for revitalization of body and soul and the exhilarating experience of desert living - the air - clean and dry, the sky - a rich and vibrant blue, the land - bountiful, the recreation - unparalleled. Many stayed to start a new life away from the turmoil and congestion of big city life, the rains of the Northwest or the winters of the Midwest and East.

They stayed because the Coachella Valley creates a vivacity for life, a feeling that lingers, a feeling that's addictive. It's been this way since man discovered this valley scarcely more than a hundred years ago.

In the Beginning   II

In the Beginning

In the beginning, the Coachella Valley's desolate expanses were foreboding, isolated and bone-dry under the blazing sun. Other than for a few Indian tribes living in the surrounding region - the Agua Caliente, Cabazon, Morongo, Augustine and the Twenty Nine Palms Indians - and a few scouting parties mapping the Southwest for a future east-west rail route, the desert in the Coachella Valley was mostly undiscovered.

Courtesy - Palm Springs Historical Society

The western portion of the valley adjacent to Mt. San Jacinto became home to the areas oldest village where Cahuilla (ka-we-ah) Native Americans settled, some ten thousand years ago.

This early settlement was an oasis in a vast expanse of desert. Situated at the base of the mountain, the village gave refuge to the early dwellers by offering the ingredient necessary to all life - water.

During the Spanish conquest, European soldiers became increasingly familiar with the vast open desert as they explored the boundaries of their new empire. They little distracted the Cahuilla Indians who made their home in the cove areas and the shaded palm canyons running with crystal clear streams that flowed year-round.

The Cahuilla Indians who lived in the area became known as the Agua Caliente (Spanish for hot water) Tribe of Cahuilla Indians, named after the discovery of one of Coachella Valley's geologic marvels - a hot mineral spring.

Courtesy - Palm Springs Historical Society

Courtesy - Palm Springs Historical Society

Courtesy - Coachella Valley Historical Society and Museum

Surrounded by waving palms, the natural spring purified and cleansed the body as it re-vitalized the soul.

This same spring continues to bubble away life's tensions the same as it did so many centuries ago, this time surrounded by modern, man-made architecture near the center of present day Palm Springs.

Modern Exploration

III

Modern Exploration
1853

The first modern exploration of the Coachella Valley was made in 1853 by professor William P. Blake and a U. S. Army survey party looking for a train route through the southwest deserts. The survey party consisted of scientists, geologists, botanists, military officers and an artist. The lithographs reproduced here were first published in 1854. They were drawn by survey party artist Charles Koppel.

Blake named this desert the Colorado, a name to describe the expanses of desert below the 3,000 foot elevation. Deserts above 3,000 feet in elevation in California are known as the Mojave deserts. In Blake's report he made a significant observation. He predicted artesian water would be found beneath the surface of the Coachella Valley. It would be thirty-five years before that prediction proved true.

(Lithographs, Courtesy - Anza Borrego Desert Natural History Association)

Lithographs made by Charles Koppel, US Army survey party artist, depicting the Coachella Valley and the dried up bottom of the Gulf of California - first published in 1854.

He noted the old beach line at Travertine Point identifying sea level of long ago. He also found tiny, spiral seashells in the sands and at the base of the mountains. The Spanish name for the shells was conchilla. A printing error in the government report mislabeled the name as coachella, a name that has become the accepted identity of the Coachella Valley.

The Blake survey party is credited with establishing a wagon route through the San Gorgonio Pass, traversing the Coachella Valley in an east/west direction. The route essentially follows Varner Road of today. The remnants of one of the Bradshaw stage stops, known as the Rock House, can still be seen near the intersection of Varner Road and Mountain View, near Desert Hot Springs.

As other survey parties continued to explore the Coachella Valley, they universally agreed:

> *"This desert is an immense, uninhabited wasteland, incapable of civilization. Even the Indians think of this desert with terror, believing dead Indian souls are condemned to wander this desert forever - in the summer without water and in winter without clothing."*

The Coming of the Railroads
IV

The Coming of the Railroads

In the mid 19th century the western movement in the United States was on, and by 1877, various rail lines connected the East and West. In the southwest deserts, steam powered locomotives needed large quantities of water to operate their engines and water sources were scarce. When crossing the vast open deserts the trains had to carry their own tank loads of water. The small rural community of Walters, now present day Mecca, became vitally important to the railroads. In need of a desert water source, the Southern Pacific Railroad Company hired the Rose Well Drilling Company to explore for water. At 196 feet below sea level, they hit a gusher of highly pressurized artesian water. Ten rail tank cars could be filled simultaneously from this one artesian well. The year - 1894.

(Courtesy Coachella Valley Historical Society & Museum)
Water Well drillers tapping into the underground aquifer

What drilling for water did was to discover the vast underground aquifer just below the surface. The aquifer, one of the largest in the state, is located below the entire Coachella Valley, from Palm Springs in the West to beneath the Salton Sea in the East. The aquifer supplies nearly all of the domestic water required for the growing population of the Coachella Valley. Snowmelt and run-off from the surrounding mountains helps replenish the aquifer.

Walters was a major *"water stop"* prior to the trains climbing up and over the pass separating the San Bernardino and San Jacinto Mountains, or crossing the vast open desert to Yuma, Arizona and beyond. The train's western destination, El Pueblo de Nuestra Señora de La Reina de Los Angeles - a struggling little village at the edge of the Pacific Ocean with a population of just a few thousand people mostly engaged in ranching and trading hides.

(Courtesy Coachella Valley Historical Society & Museum)
Storage tank adjacent to railroad tracks at Walters, later renamed Mecca

(Courtesy Coachella Valley Historical Society & Museum)

To aid western expansion, the United States Government gave odd numbered sections of land, ten miles on each side of the tracks, to the railroad. Later, even numbered sections of land were given to the Cahuilla Indians, creating the checkerboard pattern of growth so evident in the Coachella Valley. Many railroad lands were sold to the early settlers who started to inhabit the Coachella Valley.

With water diverted to the farms from the aquifer, the Coachella Valley began to produce abundant crops, year round. A marriage soon took place between the farmers and the trains, as the newly harvested crops started to be distributed all around the country.

(Courtesy Coachella Valley Historical Society & Museum)
Women packing grapes for shipment to market

(Courtesy Coachella Valley Historical Society & Museum)
Passenger rail cars at the Indio train station

The western movement was in full swing, and coming west by rail was the preferable mode of travel, replacing crossing the country by wagon train. There were so many people riding the rails that the competition for passengers traveling to California became fierce.

Southern Pacific passenger rates were reduced to a low of one dollar per trip from Missouri to Los Angeles. Many of the early colonists got off the trains in the Coachella Valley to start their new life.

(Courtesy Coachella Valley Historical Society & Museum)
Indio train station - the center of social and business activity in Indio

The People Come

V

The People Come

Slowly, as people settled into the Coachella Valley, new communities sprang up based around agriculture - Woodspur, today known as Coachella, Thermal, originally known as Kokell, Valerie Jean, Arabia, Oasis, Edom, and Walters, now present day Mecca. These first settlers to the Coachella Valley knew that with hard work, their dreams of a better life could be fulfilled. Farming began to fan out into other areas of the valley other than around Indio and Coachella. Heavy plantings of citrus and dates took place all along the northern flank of the Santa Rosas and into the Palm Springs area.

Courtesy - Palm Springs Historical Society

Courtesy - Palm Springs Historical Society

Courtesy - Palm Springs Historical Society

Farming in the Coachella Valley expanded to a hundred thousand acres of land. With irrigation water from the underground aquifer applied to the soil, the farm community prospered. Vegetables of all types were successfully planted, along with grapefruit, oranges, lemons and other fruit trees. With a virtual twelve-month growing season, Coachella Valley farm products would reach the market ahead of its competition, bringing top dollar. Because of the initial success of early Coachella Valley crops many other farmers planted the same crop the following year, looking for more *"top dollars."* Quite often, it spelled ruin as the market became over produced leading to bottomed-out prices. Because of the advantage of harvesting ahead of the competition, however, the farmers soon learned to plant and harvest their crops for *"windows of opportunity markets"* tied to transportation systems. It has always been that way in farming, even today.

In spite of the ups and down of farming, people discovered that the Coachella Valley was a delightful place to live and work. Many viewed the Coachella Valley as a land of opportunity - abundant inexpensive land, ample water, sunshine nearly year round - a paradise. The summers, however, were *"somewhat warm."*

Population expansion took a major jump after WWII. Soldiers, many who had trained for desert warfare a few miles east of Indio returned to settle down. And a constant stream of newcomers, too, began to settle into the entire valley, from Palm Springs to the west, down to the Salton Sea. Development began to spring up among the budding cove communities, too - La Quinta, originally known as Marshall's Cove, Indian Wells, Palm Desert, originally known as Sand Hole and later Palm Village, Rancho Mirage and Cathedral City, all originally nestled at the base of the Santa Rosa Mountains. Other communities that surrounded the central valley continued to add to the population growth, too - Desert Hot Springs, North Palm Springs, Sky Valley, Bermuda Dunes, Indio Hills, Thermal and Thousand Palms. The desert was growing.

Courtesy Coachella Valley Historical Society & Museum

Courtesy - Coachella Valley Water District

Courtesy - Coachella Valley Water District

Courtesy Coachella Valley Historical Society & Museum

45

(Courtesy - Historical Society of Palm Desert)
Aerial of Rancho Mirage and Palm Desert - 1950s

In the 1950s, however, Coachella Valley was still mostly open desert. True, the farming area was being settled but most builders looked at the Coachella Valley as too remote and too hot for residential development. It was during this period that Coachella Valley established the infrastructure of the valley of the future, a valley that today is meeting expectations for an exceptional way of life - an economic balance between land and water, development, agriculture, business and dynamic recreation.

Palm Springs

VI

Palm Springs
Incorporated 1938

The first permanent white settler in the Palm Springs area was Judge John Guthrie McCallum and his family who arrived in 1885. Here, he found the perfect location and healthful climate for his tubercular son. McCallum purchased land from the railroad and built an adobe home for his family. The home today on Palm Canyon Drive is headquarters of the Palm Springs Historical Society.

All Historical Photos Courtesy Palm Springs Historical Society

Judge John Guthrie McCallum, first white settler in Palm Springs

Stone lined water ditch bringing water from the Whitewater River

First citrus planting in Palm Springs

Remnants of the failed "Palmdale" development in Palm Springs

Palm Springs about 1910

After acquiring about 6,000 acres of land to start an agriculture venture, McCallum constructed the first major man-made irrigation project in Western America - a stone lined canal that captured the runoff from the snows of Mt. San Gorgonio and the Whitewater River. This first water supply for the Palm Springs area gave impetus for ongoing development in the region. At the time, Palm Springs was known as Palmdale and future development appeared promising. By the early 1890s irrigated lands were producing citrus, grapes and vegetables.

The first Coachella Valley school soon opened in Palm Springs, part of the Banning School District. The area was growing but was limited by the ability to acquire a permanent water source. It was a beginning paradise until the winter of 1893 when torrential rains washed out the irrigation ditches and the plantings. A decade of drought followed, shattering all hopes of establishing Palm Springs as a center for agriculture. The dreams of McCallum's Palm Valley Land and Water Company development folded, shattering both the dreams and the life of McCallum, who died in 1905.

Palm Springs about 1930

Palm Springs Hotel - the first of the village's resorts - 1900s

After the turn of the century, however, Palm Springs' heritage was getting a kick start - a desert resort community consisting of ten buildings, a post office, and a growing number of visitors who stayed at the first resort, the Palm Springs Hotel. Room and board cost $2.00 a night, with a discount on a weekly rate. The close-by hot springs was leased from the Cahuilla Indians by the hotel for guest use. In spite of really roughing it in early Palm Springs - no electricity, no telephones, no sidewalks, dirt roadways, free roaming donkeys - people were beginning to discover the magic of the desert.

The bustling and growing community of Los Angeles, just a hundred miles to the northwest was growing by leaps and bounds - especially the movie industry. The Coachella Valley desert served as the location for films depicting exotic locations such as Mexico, the Sahara desert and biblical locations.

Palm Canyon about 1930

El Mirador Hotel in the 1930s

The historic and renowned El Mirador Hotel tower, a landmark for Palm Springs, was completed in 1928 only to be destroyed by fire in the late eighties. It has since been rebuilt, continuing its strong identity as a landmark for the City of Palm Springs.

During WWII the hotel was purchased by the military to serve as a hospital for the rehabilitation of wounded veterans returning from fighting the war in the Pacific Theater of Operations. The new hospital was the first complex in the desert to have air conditioning. Most businesses throughout the desert closed their doors during the summer in an attempt to escape the almost unbearable heat.

Henry Ford was changing the old buckboard and horse drawn wagons for transportation into a thriving business and everyone wanted to own the new contraption - the Model T Ford. A major problem was that there were very few roads in the Coachella Valley other than unpaved ruts in the ground. The budding community of Palm Springs became a stopover for the *"horseless carriages"* as they explored the desert's open spaces, especially the sand dunes near Yuma, Arizona, home of California's first freeway system - a wooden plank highway.

Horseless carriage road race from Los Angeles to Palm Springs - 1920s

Palms Springs, one of the oldest villages on the western continent, is more than a quaint little desert village in the shadow of Mt. San Jacinto. Within a two-hour drive from most major cities in southern California, Palm Springs has become a mecca for winter tourists. Because of its many attractions, it also serves as a major destination for visitors from around the world, as well as the convention headquarters for companies who have found Palm Springs a *"destination of choice"* all through the year. Golf, tennis and swimming blend easily with elegant and diverse shopping, museums, restaurants, visitor attractions and entertainment centers. Palm Springs is a community that, once visited, will be remembered for a lifetime. **PS - I Love You -** says it all.

America's First Freeway

VII

America's First Freeway
1914 - 1926

From the Coachella Valley to Yuma, Arizona, the desert lands were barely more than dusty, rutted washboards. It was tough traversing the roadways through the desert, especially the roads adjacent to the Salton Sea. Trains still carried most of the traveling public. But the Model T was finding its way into the heart and life of the American public and people wanted to travel.

To the southeast of the Salton Sea lay the remains of the dried up sea bottom of the Gulf of California known as the Algodones Sand Dunes. After the Gulf of California became separated and the water in Ancient Lake Cahuilla evaporated, the prevailing winds blew the fine sand particles into huge dunes reaching heights of over three hundred feet. Conventional roadways built over the sand dunes were constantly being covered with sand almost a fast as they could be built.

In 1914, a wooden roadway was constructed with 2" by 12" wooden planks laid parallel to each other the width of a car. They were lashed together with cross ties. It was almost impossible for motorists to navigate the planks and the *"roadway"* became useless.

In 1916, however, an improved wooden roadway was constructed of 4" thick planks lashed together with cross ties and bound together with steel straps. The full-width wooden sections were moved into position by teams of horses. The sections were built just over one car wide with double sections placed every quarter mile or so, allowing cars traveling in opposite directions to pass. If the sand covered the planks, they could easily be lifted and repositioned. The road was used for ten years until roadway engineering improved and a repositioned asphalt highway was built.

Remnants of the early *"plank roadway"* system can be seen today in Imperial County, adjacent to Interstate 8 in the Algodones Dunes. Some have called this roadway over the sand the beginning of California's freeway system.

Indio
Incorporated 1939

It was water that opened the door to agriculture in the Coachella Valley. The City of Indio and the surrounding desert lands became the center of activity. Trains traveling through the Coachella Valley were on the increase and whether traveling east or west, all trains stopped at Indio. The Southern Pacific Hotel built adjacent to the railroad tracks was Indio's focal center. Passengers could take a meal at the hotel while train crews switched over to a fresh crew. Being at the crossroads of the desert, the trains brought people to help settle the land. Although most passengers were from the east or mid west on their way to Los Angeles, many traveled to the Coachella Valley and the warm desert climate to recuperate from respiratory diseases.

Historical Photos Courtesy of Coachella Valley Historical Society & Museum

Life in Indio then was primitive. There were no phones, no electricity, travel was by carriage or buckboards and the roads were unpaved and often flooded. The roads were so bad that if you wanted to travel from Indio to Mecca, a distance of ten miles, you would have to plan to take nearly a full day for the trip.

Roughing it in Indio was an understatement - it was mostly undeveloped, open desert, hot as h--- in the summer and often bitterly cold during winter. One report on the climate of the Coachella Valley stated, *"the climate in the hot months is not one in which a sane person would select in which to spend the summer."* Many who came to Indio, however, thought of the area as their new start - a true, land of opportunity. Many still do.

Soon the City of Indio and the surrounding farm community became partners. The farmers needed a rail hub to send their produce to market and Indio became that hub. Growing farm crops in the Coachella Valley on the fertile land with ample water soon earned the Coachella Valley the distinction of being called *"the fresh vegetable and salad bowl of the nation."* Fresh fruits and vegetables grown in the Coachella Valley graced the tables in most American cities. Sending produce to the Eastern markets often took ten days by train. Scheduled stops to ice-up the rail cars were made all along the route. Most often, however, you just took your chances in shipping produce to the East, especially during the summer.

Palm fronds cover the roof of an early Indio home helping to reduce the stifling heat

During the summer it was not only hot in the Coachella Valley - it was very hot. In order to sleep at night, you would have to dip a bed sheet in the bath tub full of water, ring it out, spread it on the bed and crawl onto it. By the time it dried out, with a little bit of luck, you would hopefully be asleep. Hopefully!

Indio was the crew change station for the railroaders. Here the railroads created unusual housing facilities for their crews. Wooden frame structures were covered with sheets of galvanized iron and then overlaid with burlap. Water was trickled onto the burlap, cooling the metal, and cooling the interior. Railroaders named them *"desert submarines."* The temperature inside the structure dropped about twenty degrees Fahrenheit, allowing for a good night's sleep for the hot and tired crews.

Typical water cooled "desert submarine" used for sleeping by railroaders when switching crews at the Indio station

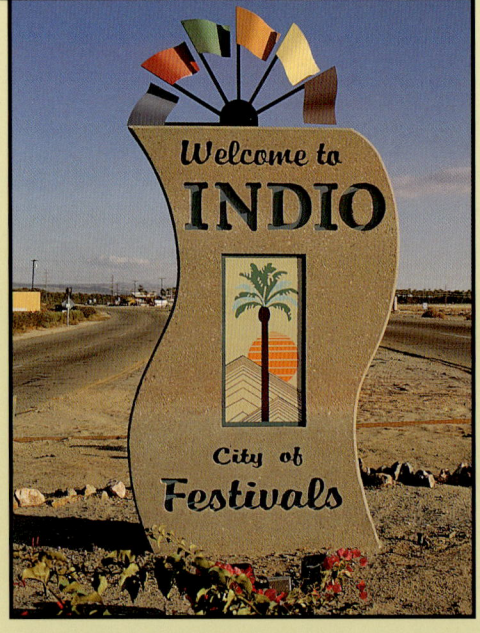

Over the years, Indio has become known as the *"city of festivals."* Starting with the Indio Southwest Arts Festival with world-renown artists displaying their creations, it follows with the Riverside County Fair and National Date Festival where the community and the county honors its agriculture heritage amid the hoops and hollers of a county fair like no other. Festivals take place all through the year - the Indio Desert Circuit Horse Show attracting equestrian jumpers from Europe and South America, world-class polo takes place during the winter and into spring, Indian Pow Wow's, golf's infamous Skins Game, Independence Day Celebrations and culminating with a most unusual event in early December, the International Tamale Festival.

Indio's influence in the Coachella Valley cannot be underestimated. At the turn of the century there were only two major communities in the Coachella Valley - Indio and Palm Springs. A two-lane dirt and gravel road (Hwy 111) tied the two together. As the people came, they soon discovered the magic that marks Indio as a special place. People are still discovering Indio, as well as the entire Coachella Valley - and they're still coming. The future of the Coachella Valley identifies the lands in the lower eastern and southern areas of the valley beyond Indio as prime for dynamic expansion and population growth.

Indio's ambassadors giving out dates to Richfield gas station customers

A drive around Indio today reveals "building size" murals depicting Indio's early history

Coachella

IX

Coachella
Incorporated 1946

Known as *"The City of Eternal Sunshine,"* Coachella spreads across the dried up sea bottom of the former Gulf of California at 62 feet below sea level. Just prior to the twentieth century, the land was isolated, barren and covered in mesquite trees. It was desolate and forlorn - but with unseen potential. As the railroads began to cross the valley, things were changing.

Courtesy- (Coachella Valley Water District)
Mesquite wood gathering was a major business in early Coachella

Courtesy- (Coachella Valley Water District)
Trains were loaded with mesquite wood and shipped to Los Angeles

As rail activity increased, a small depot and siding was built south of Indio to accommodate the trains. The land was heavily covered with mesquite trees, providing an almost unlimited supply of wood to ship to Los Angeles or to burn aboard the trains, turning water into steam to power the locomotives. For lack of a better name, the siding became known as Woodspur and it soon became a focal center of activity. At first a wooden water tower was installed, then water mains. Streets were graded, a few homes were built and businesses associated with the railroad started to serve the area.

Courtesy-(Coachella Valley Water Water District)
Grapefruit Blvd., Coachella in the 1930's

By 1901, a company was formed for the development of Woodspur into a viable community. Early settlers and native Americans who lived and worked in the area called the entire region Cahuilla Valley, a name that the locals felt could and should be improved on. Since the lands in the area were nothing more than dried up sea bottom containing many tiny seashells, known as conchilla or conchas, the city fathers decided to rename the community. The regional name was changed to Coachella Valley, and Woodspur was given the name of Coachella. The name change became officially approved in 1909.

Courtesy- (Coachella Valley Water District)
Cantaloupe field workers resting after a day in the sun

Courtesy- (Coachella Valley Water District)
Early steam powered water drilling rig

Courtesy- (Coachella Valley Water District)
Downtown Coachella in the 1930s

Courtesy- (Coachella Valley Water District)
Coachella Valley baseball champions - 1913

Courtesy- (Coachella Valley Water District)
First schoolhouse in Coachella

In the beginning, electric power was limited to those families who maintained their own diesel generators. By 1914, the first installation of electrical service began when electric service was extended from San Bernardino into the Coachella Valley. Caleb Cook, an early rancher in the budding date industry, filled his off hours from farming by helping Coachella residents wire their homes and ranches for electricity. As the region became electrified, one of the biggest sellers at the hardware stores was electric fans offering a little relief from the warm summers. It would be another forty years before air conditioning would begin to help residents through the summer months.

Courtesy- (Coachella Valley Water District)
Street flooding in Coachella in the 1930s

Courtesy- (Coachella Valley Water District)
Huntington and Smythe store in downtown Coachella - 1909

Coachella's location in the center of the valley destined it to become a main commercial center for the growing and distribution of farm products. Today, produce processing plants work throughout the year meeting the needs of produce buyers from around the country and around the world. As the entire valley continues to expand its population with numbers unimagined just a few years ago, the future of the dynamic agriculture industry, the valley's number two economic power house, holds great promise for a continuing bright future.

Courtesy- (Coachella Valley Water District)
Fresh picked corn on its way to market

The City of Coachella, too, is the center of the labor force that serves the needs of the farming activity. About 98% of Coachella's population is of Hispanic origin and one can see and feel the strength of a family oriented people who reside in this community.

Because of the dynamic expanse of agriculture, this region of the Coachella Valley is often referred as *"the green end of the valley."* If it can be grown, chances are that it can be grown in the Coachella Valley.

The Date Industry

X

The Date Industry

The date palm is an old native tree from the arid Middle East and North Africa, where it has been growing for thousands of years. Date trees from these regions provided food, feed, fiber and shelter for nomadic people since before biblical times.

Dates were introduced to many regions of California by Spanish explorers who planted the trees adjacent to the Missions they established throughout California. The Missions were built close to the sea to take advantage of ocean commerce ruled by Spain in the 16th and 17th centuries. Date trees were a reminder of home to the Spanish explorers. The date tree plantings near the cooler ocean climate, however, restricted the trees to being decorative only. Dates, in order to be grown commercially, require a long, hot and arid growing season to mature and ripen, like the climate found in the Coachella Valley.

Courtesy Coachella Valley Historical Society & Museum

Courtesy Coachella Valley Historical Society & Museum

The first importing of dates to the Coachella Valley was made in 1890 by the U.S. Department of Agriculture. These early plantings, many of which were grown from seed, produced inferior fruit or no fruit at all because they were mostly male trees. Only female trees produce fruit while the male date tree provides the pollen for fertilization of the flowers. In commercial plantings throughout the Coachella Valley, one male tree is planted to each acre of approximately fifty female trees. Pollen from the male tree is gathered and then *"powder puffed"* onto the female blooms assuring a high degree of fertilization. One old male tree, King David, located at the Oasis Date Garden, is still going strong doing his thing. It is believed that King David fertilized tens of thousands of female date trees in the Coachella Valley.

KING DAVID

A venerable male date palm, planted before 1912. One male palm produces enough pollen to polinate 40-50 female trees. Only the female produces fruit.

In 1900, the United States Department of Agriculture brought Deglet Noor offshoots from Algeria to the Coachella Valley. The following year, offshoots of many different varieties arrived from Iraq and Egypt marking the beginning of California's date industry. It wasn't until 1927, however, that the Medjool date was introduced to the Coachella Valley. The Medjool variety has remained a favorite because of its size (the largest), texture and taste. Individual date varieties, however, have their own distinctive qualities. Many are used in processed foods such as cereals and baking products. Many are eaten like candy from freshly packed assortments. A date crystal shake on a warm afternoon offers refreshment beyond description.

(Courtesy Coachella Valley Historical Society & Museum)
Early date farmer Bernard G. Johnson and his newly planted date offshoots - 1904

(Courtesy Coachella Valley Historical Society & Museum)
Indio newspaper headline - 1915

Date trees require extensive care all through the year. Dead branches must be removed from each tree, blossoms must be tied together to protect them from the wind, and once blooming occurs, the flowers must be fertilized by powdering male pollen onto the blooms.

The bunches of newly fertilized flowers are covered to protect them from summer moisture. When harvesting, the covers are removed, the date bunches are cut and gently lowered to the ground. Ag personnel must climb each tree a minimum of six to eight times a year to service a date tree. Sixty to seventy foot tall trees make the process somewhat labor intensive.

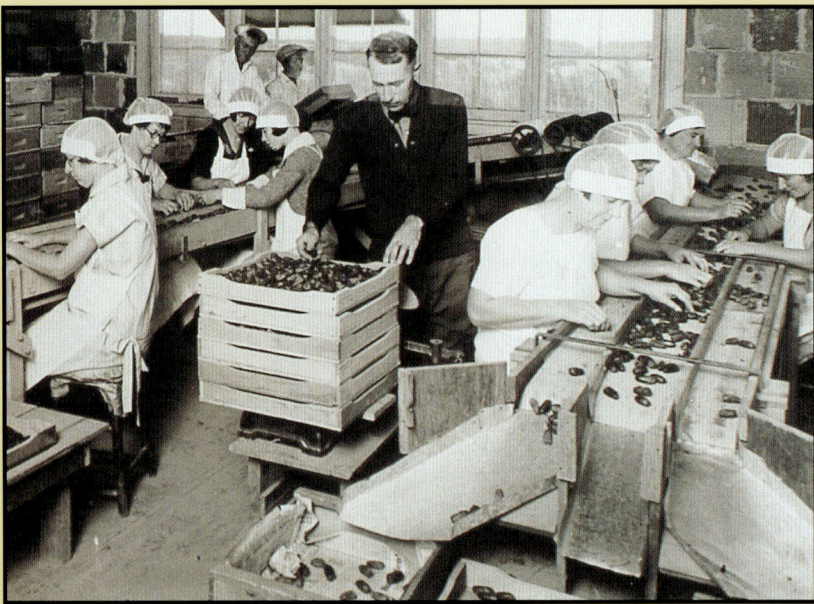

(Courtesy Coachella Valley Historical Society & Museum)
Early date industry packing fruit for market

(Courtesy Coachella Valley Historical Society & Museum)
Grading dates by hand to ensure quality. Women still dominate date grading.

Coachella Valley date orchards represent 95% of all of the date palm plantings in the United States. A visit to the annual Indio National Date Festival will help visitors understand the importance of the date industry to the Coachella Valley.

The Salton Sea   XI

The Salton Sea

In the geologically past, most of California was once part of a larger body of water extending north through the San Joaquin Valley to near Sacramento. A great geological rise of the lands lifted the Coachella Valley and the surrounding mountains. Later, a down folding of the land, extending southeast from the San Gorgonio Pass, created the Coachella and Imperial Valleys. Over millions of years, silt and mud carried down the Colorado River were deposited in the Imperial Valley region, creating a land bridge that parted the Gulf of California. The newly created inland sea extended into the upper Coachella Valley producing the present day *"bath tub ring"* along the base of the Santa Rosa Mountains.

This first body of water in the Coachella and Imperial Valleys was given the name, Lake Le Conte. A more familiar name, however, is now identified with that body of water - Ancient Lake Cahuilla. After time, this first inland ocean/lake eventually evaporated revealing the bottom of the Gulf of California.

Millennium after millennium, as the Colorado River raced to the Gulf of California, it often changed its course, sending fresh water and silt into the lowest depression in the valley. Here, the water would rest until the river changed course again, allowing the water to evaporate - time and time again. As the silt rushed down the Colorado River it settled into the lower reaches of California raising the level of the land.

Crusted salt deposits near the edge of the Salton Sea.

In the upper Coachella Valley, coarser, sandy alluvial deposits from the Whitewater River and the canyons of the Coachella Valley also started to raise the level of the Coachella Valley. This was the early beginning of the underground aquifer storage basin that today provides domestic water in the Coachella Valley.

The Salton Sink, the lowest depression in the valley prior to the present day Salton Sea, saw numerous short-lived seas as the result of the Colorado River changing it course. About fifteen hundred years ago, the lake had evaporated once again and remained dry until man attempted to alter nature. While the Salton Sink depression is a geologic abnormality, the Salton Sea is the product of an error by men interested in developing farming.

(Courtesy - Imperial Irrigation District)
Broken head-works that diverted Colorado River water into the Salton Sink

(Courtesy - Imperial Irrigation District)
Colorado River water flooding the Imperial and Coachella Valleys

In the late 1800's, farmers of the Imperial Valley had discovered the rich alluvial soils washed out of the Grand Canyon and were producing crops, year round. Diversion structures dug into the side of the Colorado River carried the irrigation water in earthen canals to the farms. The water, however, was so loaded with silt that the canals soon plugged up, and new diversion structures had to be build.

Water was again being diverted from a structure cut into the side of the Colorado River on the Mexican side of the border. From south of Yuma, the water traveled in earthen canals through the Republic of Mexico to the Imperial Valley farmlands.

Then, in 1905, disaster struck. A rampaging Colorado River flood broke through the head works of the irrigation canal and flowed to the lowest depression of the land - the Salton Sink. For more than two years the Colorado River changed from flowing south to flowing north, creating the present day Salton Sea. It took more than two years to close the break in the head-works and return the Colorado River back into its former channel. Devastation was extensive. The water of the newly formed Salton Sea extended up to the small community of Mecca, inundating nearly 350,000 acres of land.

(Courtesy - Coachella Valley Water District)

(Courtesy - Coachella Valley Water District)

(Courtesy Coachella Valley Historical Society & Museum)
Flooded railroad trestle at the newly formed Salton Sea

(Courtesy - Imperial Irrigation District)
It took two years to finally re-direct the river back into the old channel

The Salton Sea today covers over 380 square miles of surface water. Its width varies from 9 to 15 miles and is about 35 miles long. The sea contains 115 miles of shoreline. The Salton Sea varies in depth with the gentle valley slope to about 51 feet deep.

Because of the abundant fish life in the Sea, the waters have become home to numerous bird species such as the yellow footed gull, Caspian terns, Canadian geese, Pintail ducks, Snow geese, Blue Heron and many others.

The Salton Sea maintains one of the most productive fisheries in the state and offers good fishing, year-round. Some of the more fished for species are the Orangemouth Corvina, Croaker, Sargo and Tilapia.

By federal law, the Salton Sea has become the depository of drainage, waste and surface water from Imperial Valley, the Coachella Valley and parts of Mexico. Through evaporation (leaving the minerals and salts to become concentrated), the Salton Sea is about one-third saltier than the ocean.

The water inflows, however, help maintain the sea's surface level at about 232 feet below sea level. Annual evaporation of the Salton Sea, due to temperature extremes, is estimated at about six feet a year. Without the fresh water inflows from the farms and from Mexico, the Salton Sea would soon become more saline, incapable of maintaining fish life, and the sea would be reduced to a fraction of its present size.

Satellite view of the Coachella Valley, the Salton Sea and Imperial Valley from space.

The Salton Sea at sunset - California's largest body of water.

Coachella Valley Goes to War XII

Coachella Valley Goes to War

East of the Coachella Valley and spread out across the deserts of California and Arizona, World War II U.S. Army training camps conditioned tens of thousands of soldiers under the direction of General George C. Patton, known as *"old blood and guts."*

Historical Photos Courtesy General Patton Museum
General George C. Patton

The training areas were centered at numerous camps from the Mexican border north into California, Nevada and Arizona. Here, under adverse desert conditions, American soldiers trained on how to become combat ready. At Camp Young near Chiriaco Summit, about forty miles east of Indio, some 25,000 soldiers at a time were undergoing deadly desert warfare training. Training received at Camp Young served the soldiers well as they battled the Germans all across North Africa and Europe.

Ten percent of the Camp Young soldiers were given passes every ten days to take leave from the rigorous training. Indio, the closest community to Camp Young, played host to a large percentage of the 2,500 soldiers who were looking for a little R & R - every night of the week. In one sense, it was like an invasion. Downtown Indio at the time consisted of little more than two sides of one block. Located here was a single theater, a few restaurants, a newspaper that appeared weekly, a tiny department store and lots and lots of open farmland surrounding all.

Every night of the week thousands of soldiers rushed to Indio looking for recreation. On Saturday nights there was no space on the sidewalks for walking as the soldiers spilled over onto the curbs. But in spite of the crowded conditions, the citizens of Indio responded with warmth and hospitality. Many a soldier was treated as family, often spending a Sunday or holiday dinner with the residents of Indio.

When the Desert Training Center was closed in 1944, Italian POW's began the dismantling process. Surplus buildings were sold to valley residents and recycled into homes and office buildings. Many of these familiar rectangular shaped buildings are still visible today throughout the Coachella Valley serving as a reminder of the war years.

The Movie Colony   XIII

The Movie Colony

The Hollywood movie colony, too, discovered the Coachella Valley, not only for making movies, but for rest and relaxation. In the late 1930's, 40's and 50's, movie stars flocked to the desert. Just a few hours by car, they came from the Los Angeles metropolitan area to relax from the demands of movie making, and to party, party, party.

Historical Photos Courtesy The Racquet Club & Spa, Palm Springs

Robert Wagner & Natalie Wood

Entrance to the Racquet Club & Spa - 1930s

They headquartered at Charlie Farrell's Racquet Club Hotel and Spa in Palm Springs where they swam and played tennis. Partying throughout the Coachella Valley desert by the movie colony has continued unabated through the years. It's not clear if the movie stars came to the Coachella Valley for the sun and clean desert air or the partying - perhaps for both.

Harpo Marx

John Garfield

Rita Hayworth

William Powell

Rosalind Russell

Kirk Douglas

Jeanne Crain

Charlie Farrell, owner of The Racquet Club

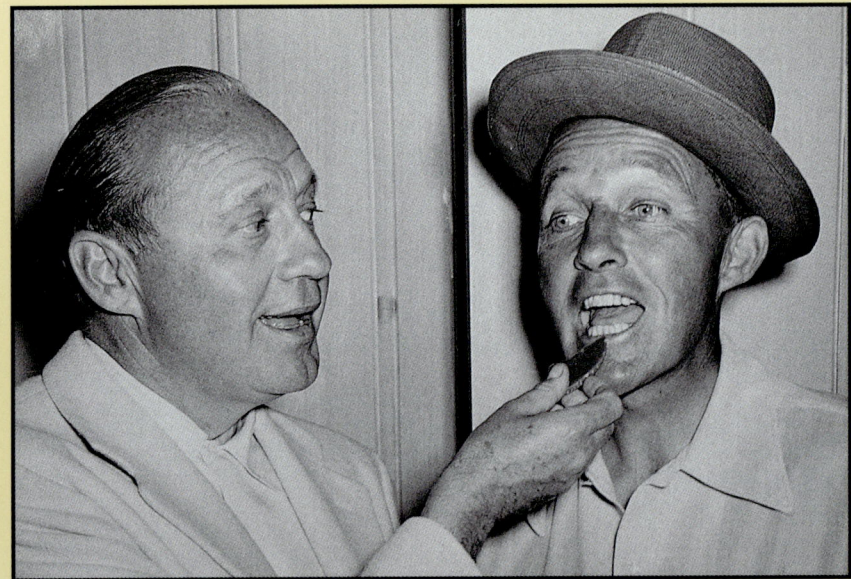
Jack Benny & Bing Crosby

Starting with the Racquet Club as headquarters of the movie colony in the 1930s, the entire Coachella Valley soon became the site of first and second homes to many leading stars - Bob Hope, Bing Crosby, Edgar Bergan, Frank Morgan, Ginger Rogers, Harold Lloyd, Dinah Shore, George Montgomery, Frank Sinatra, and many, many others. Even today, it is not uncommon to rub elbows with celebrities and other famous people anywhere in the desert.

Coachella Valley Water

XIV

Coachella Valley Water

Water means many things to many people. Water can lead to prosperity, to feuding, to survival, or in its absence, death. In this part of the great southwest desert, water is the critical element that sustains every aspect of our existence. Water is Coachella Valley's life blood.

(Courtesy - Coachella Valley Water District)
Water is released into the Whitewater River from the Colorado River Aqueduct to help recharge the aquifer

An often heard phrase attributed to those who are involved in the water business, *"whisky's for drinking and water's for fighting."* The Coachella Valley exists because of water. This is a land that receives a scant 2 to 4 inches of rain a year, often none at all. Contrast that with the rainforests of the State of Washington which receive over 400 inches of rain a year. Now you know why so many people from the Northwest like to spend the winter in the Coachella Valley. Washingtonians and Oregonians say it is impossible to get a tan at home - they just rust.

After the discovery of the underground aquifer by the railroads in 1875, it has been the availability of water that has guided and controlled the destiny of the Coachella Valley. Early on after the discovery of the aquifer, the farmers came, turning a dry and desolate desert into a land of prosperity. But it did not happen overnight.

Courtesy - Coachella Valley Water District

Courtesy - Coachella Valley Water District

Courtesy - Coachella Valley Water District

Courtesy - Coachella Valley Water District

(Courtesy - Coachella Valley Water District)
Flooding in downtown Indio - 1916

Periodic flooding throughout the Coachella Valley after the turn of the century gave rise to the establishment of the Coachella Valley Water District in 1918. The desert lands were mostly flat, so when the infrequent rains came, the area often flooded. One of the first orders of business for the CVWD was storm water protection. Massive earthen dikes were built to direct storm water from farm and residential areas. Diversion dikes and concrete channels were constructed in the cove areas to direct the water into the newly enlarged Whitewater Storm Channel. Storm waters, if heavy enough, might find their way to the Salton Sea, or just sink into the ground.

It wasn't until 1960, however, that most domestic water services came under the control of the CVWD. Many of the early settlers and beginning communities in the valley provided water to local residents from their own wells. Over the years most of the independent water providers elected to join ranks with the CVWD, which now serves domestic water to about 80% of the valley and 100% to the farming areas.

(Courtesy - Coachella Valley Water District)
Storm water runoff devastated the farm fields

(Courtesy - Coachella Valley Water District)
Early construction of the 124 mile long Coachella branch of the All-American canal ending at the terminal reservoir, Lake Cahuilla

Irrigation water for the farms was also being pumped from the underground aquifer. A project to bring Colorado River water to irrigate Coachella Valley farms actually got its beginning in the 1930's as a part of the Boulder Canyon Reclamation Project. The project included the transportation of water by gravity from the Colorado River via the All-American Canal and a branch canal to bring water into the Coachella Valley. Delayed by the war, the Coachella Branch of the All-American Canal was completed in 1948 allowing distribution of Colorado River water to every 40 acres of land in the farming area of the Coachella Valley. This new source of irrigation water reduced the demand of pumping water from the underground aquifer.

(Courtesy - Coachella Valley Water District)
When completed in 1948, Colorado River water was delivered to every forty acres of farm land in the Coachella Valley

Imperial Dam on the Colorado River near Yuma

Water flows by gravity to the Coachella Valley

Canal passes open desert and lush farm fields

Lake Cahuilla terminal reservoir in La Quinta

Colorado River water is released at Imperial Dam to then travel 153 miles to the Coachella Valley, arriving at Lake Cahuilla in La Quinta, the terminal reservoir. Most of the farm community switched from pumping water from the aquifer to irrigating their fields with water from the Colorado River. A few farms located on the hip of the mountains, however, still pump water from the underground. Most Coachella Valley farms today irrigate their crops using micro-irrigation drip systems, saving both water and money, while increasing crops yield.

The entire Coachella Valley is served domestic water from the aquifer beneath the valley. It's a closed and protected system, virtually impenetrable from contamination.

The CVWD water delivery system is monitored and controlled from the headquarters facility in the City of Coachella. In the control room, computer controlled sensing systems are displayed for operators to keep the entire system in balance, 24-7, matching supply with demand.

(Courtesy-Coachella Valley Water District)
Skilled operators at CVWD headquarters control the flow of water to the entire service area

Palm Springs' Desert Water Agency developed its own water system early on by initially capturing the snowmelt from Mt. San Jacinto. As the Palm Springs community grew, pumping water from the underground aquifer was initiated to supplement the snowmelt runoff. The Desert Water Agency serves Palm Springs and a portion of Cathedral City.

Both water districts reclaim wastewater that is used to irrigate golf courses and municipal greenbelt areas. Some twenty-five million gallons a day of reclaimed water are processed and re-distributed throughout the valley. The distribution of reclaimed water flows through a separate piping system that is identifiable by its purple color.

Water is the life blood in the Coachella Valley and everyone is encouraged to use water wisely.

More than twenty-five million gallons of wastewater are reclaimed every day throughout the Coachella Valley

Reclaimed water is distributed to golf courses and greenbelts across the Coachella Valley

Desert Hot Springs

XV

Desert Hot Springs
Incorporated 1963

Although Desert Hot Springs was incorporated as a municipality in 1963, the community actually got its start shortly after 1900 when it became home to nine families clinging to a meager existence in the desert. The single most difficult task was obtaining water which was available only at the railroad station at Garnet, a fourteen mile round trip. Weighing over seven pounds per gallon, only limited amounts of water could be hand carried back to the home sites, and it required three round trips per week to obtain enough water to sustain life.

One of those early pioneers was Cabot Yerxa (yerk-sa). He acquired a 160 acre homestead in the open desert for the ridiculous sum of $10.00. His constant companion and trusted friend was "Merry Christmas," a burro who eased the chore of carrying water and building supplies which he scavenged throughout the desert.

(Courtesy - Cabot Yerxa Museum, Desert Hot Springs)
Cabot Yerxa's home overlooking his 160 acre homestead atop Miracle Hill

Digging for a new water source, Cabot discovered water on his property. Only problem was that the water temperature was 132 degrees Fahrenheit, which was OK for bathing but too mineralized for drinking. Drilling another well just 600 yards away on his own land he discovered cold, potable water. The Cabot property straddled an earthquake fault. Both hot and cold water became abundantly available to continue homesteading on the newly named property, Miracle Hill.

(Courtesy - Cabot Yerxa Museum, Desert Hot Springs)
Cabot Yerxa, descendant of the Cabots of Boston, died in 1965

(Courtesy - Cabot Yerxa Museum, Desert Hot Springs)
Cabot and his Indian friend at the 35 room Hopi style pueblo

For more than twenty years, Cabot hand-built his home, a 35 room four level, Hopi Indian style pueblo. Cabot died in 1965, leaving the pueblo unfinished. The pueblo today has been designated a Riverside County Historical site and is one of the most unusual buildings in the Coachella Valley. Cabot Yerxa's home, now a museum, is open for visitors and artists on weekends.

Located adjacent to the Pueblo is a 43 foot tall giant redwood monument, sculptured by Peter Toth from a 750 year old Sequoia redwood which was felled by lightning. The section used for the monument weighs more than 20 tons, is 8 feet in diameter and 22 feet long. Toth created his Indian Memorial to bring attention to the plight of all Native Americans.

(Courtesy - Two Bunch Palms, Desert Hot Springs)
Stone house, once owned by gangster, Al Capone.

A few miles east of downtown Desert Hot Springs, is the Two Bunch Palms Resort and Spa, a spectacular natural setting nestled among an oasis of hot springs and luxurious desert plants. The facility is designed to magically transform human spirits into a higher state of being. Like Cabot Yerxa's property, the Spa sits atop an earthquake fault providing a continuous stream of hot, mineral water that flows through the property.

Prior to becoming a spa resort, the gangster Al Capone owned Two Bunch Palms. He built a home beneath the palms where he was able to maintain surveillance over the open desert. Escape tunnels allowed him to avoid capture from his enemies, or the police. The Capone home, as well as other luxurious accommodations beneath the palms are available for visitors to experience what many consider one of the five best spas in the world.

(Courtesy - Two Bunch Palms, Desert Hot Springs)
Two Bunch Palms hot mineral springs, considered to be one of the five best spas in the world

The discovery of hot, mineralized water beneath this desert helped turn Desert Hot Springs with its mineral bath houses and therapeutic pool facilities into a thriving residential community. Desert Hot Springs is a community and vacation destination offering more than just sun and clean air to both visitors and residents alike.

(Courtesy - Two Bunch Palms, Desert Hot Springs)
One of the major groupings of palms at Two Bunch Palms

Joshua Tree National Park　　XVI

Joshua Tree National Park

With the creation of Joshua Tree National Park, this unusually beautiful desert situated on 800,000 acres is now accessible for visitors from around the world. It's just a short drive to the park from the Coachella Valley - a round trip of about 125 miles. The park encompasses some of the most dramatic geologic formations found in any desert. Mile high Keys View, overlooking the Coachella Valley, offers spectacular panoramas from Mt. San Jacinto to the Salton Sea. Whether you're a resident or just visiting, a trip through this most unusual national park will be an experience to cherish.

For all its harshness, these desert lands offer surprising variety and complexity. Joshua Tree is an extremely fragile land that will capture your imagination.

Desert vegetation lies dormant through most of the year, anxiously awaiting the mild weather and moisture that will trigger a new growth cycle resulting in a profusion of vibrant colors and textures.

The life force is patient in Joshua Tree National Park.

Joshua Tree National Park is actually comprised of two distinct deserts and its two distinct ecosystems whose characteristics are determined primarily by elevation. Below 3,000 feet, the lands are known as the Colorado Desert and are dominated by the creosote bushes, stands of ocotillo and cholla cactus. The higher, moister and slightly cooler reaches of the park above the 3,000 foot elevation are known as the Mojave Desert. This is the special habitat of the Joshua tree, providing dramatic contrast to the arid surroundings. These undisciplined trees grow amongst rock formations that were created when molten liquid oozed upward from deep within the earth, and cooled while still below the surface. Time and erosion sculpted these outcroppings over the next 100 million years. Standing like islands in a desolate sea, the Joshua trees and the rock formations provide dramatic contrast in one of nature's most unusual deserts.

(Courtesy Joshua Tree National Park)
Early Joshua Tree miners and their faithful mules

In the late 1800s explorers, cattlemen and miners came to these lands to raise cattle and search for gold. They left behind the remnants of their ventures - Lost Horse and Desert Queen mines and the Desert Queen ranch. The gold mines are accessible by a walking trail at the end of a dirt road. The Ranch may be visited during regularly scheduled guided tours that take you through some of the park's most entrancing desert landscape.

(Courtesy Joshua Tree National Park)
Entrance to the Lost Horse Mine

View of the Coachella Valley

Joshua Tree National Park provides a space for finding freedom from everyday routines, space for self-discovery, and a refuge for the human spirit.

Ocotillo in full bloom, one of the most spectacular desert plants

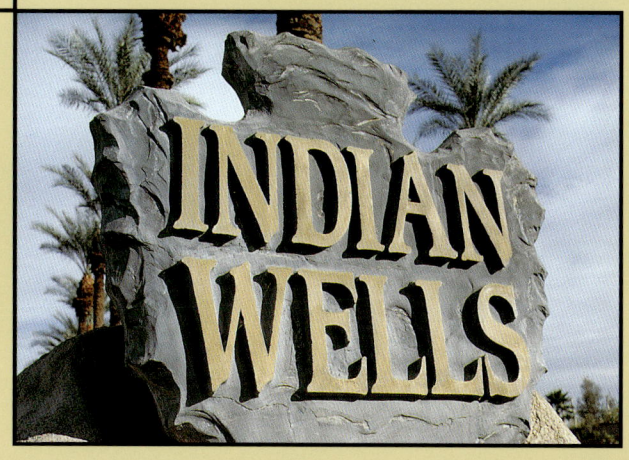

Indian Wells
Incorporated 1967

The history of Indian Wells dates back to the mid 18th century when the area was identified on early maps as the site of an old well for which the city is named. In actuality, there were three major wells in the Coachella Valley to serve early travelers. The wells were seventeen miles apart, or a day's travel by foot. One well was located on the Torres Martinez Indian Reservation, one in Palm Springs and one near the intersection of Miles and Washington, in present day Indian Wells.

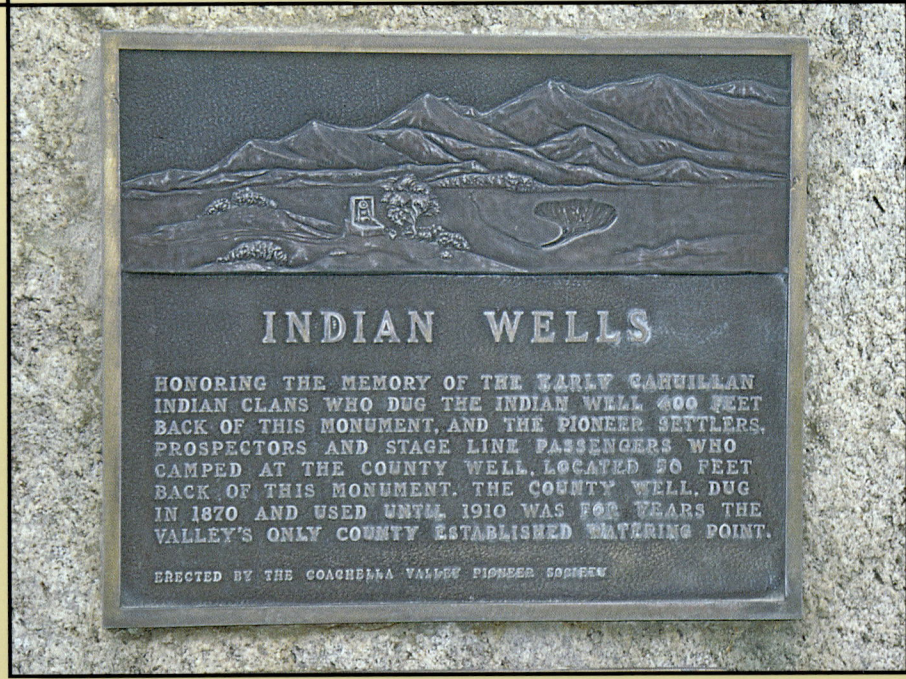

Arrowheads and broken pieces of pottery found nearby suggest that the well sites were inhabited on and off for thousands of years. The well and the surrounding thickets were called kavinic, which means *"water hole"* in the Cahuilla language.

(Courtesy - City of Indian Wells)
Original hand dug Indian well near Miles Ave and Washington St.

The first white people who passed through this area many years later identified the Miles/Washington well site as *"Indian Well."* The City of Indian Wells is named for this early well which was located at the cross roads for early travelers in the Coachella Valley.

(Courtesy - Historical Society of Palm Desert)
Travelers watering their horses at the Indian well site

Bradshaw Trail travelers resting at a watering hole - 1896 (Courtesy - Historical Society of Palm Desert)

In 1943 Cahuilla Indian Chief Francisco Patencio described the ancient well:

> "At Indian wells, the water ran from the ground, a good well. Very fine clumps of palm trees grew around it, the site of where the first palm trees grew. But the water was slowly dying. This was when the Indians had to dig deeper for the water. One side had steps going down to the water. Different Cahuilla Indian tribes were served by the water and each claimed adjacent thickets for themselves. When the harvest in the surrounding fields was ripe, all the tribes came to collect their beans and to celebrate."

The Bradshaw Stage Line created a stop at the well site, and through the years it served many who were exploring the Southwest deserts. An Army survey party in 1875 commented on the potential for growth of the Coachella Valley:

"The unfortunate climate to which portions of the Southwest is at present treated by the hand of nature is likely to retard its rapid settlement, even if water were plentifully available. The soils, however, are of a fertile nature, needing only moisture to be made productive."

(Courtesy - Historical Society of Palm Desert)
Riverside County Historical site marker of the original Indian well for which the city of Indian Wells is named

In the early 1900's settlers began trickling into the Coachella Valley lured by the increasingly accessible water supply, the capacity of the soil for growing a variety of crops and by the early success of the fledgling date industry. One of the first settlers in Indian Wells was William Blair, who along with his son, homesteaded a tract a land in the area.

Caleb Cook, for whom Cook Street is named, moved to Indian Wells in 1913 and became one of the early pioneers by establishing the first sizeable Deglet Noor date garden. His ranch was a showplace.

(Courtesy - Historical Society of Palm Desert)
Date rancher Caleb Cook, for which Cook Street is named, holding a six foot rattler

(Courtesy - City of Indian Wells)
Blair brothers operating water drilling rig - early 1900s

(Courtesy - City of Indian Wells)
First farm in Indian Wells at the turn of the century owned by William Blair

The area remained primarily a farming region until the early 1950's when the Coachella Valley's first golf course was built in the area. Not to be outdone, the El Dorado Country Club and Golf Course was dedicated in 1957, followed immediately by the Indian Wells Country Club and Golf Course.

(Courtesy - Historical Society of Palm Desert)
Aerial view of Indian Wells in the 1950s

(Courtesy - Historical Society of Palm Desert)
Looking west past Indian Wells from the intersection of Hwy 111 and Washington

Through difficult negotiations, Indian Wells was finally incorporated as a municipality in 1967, California's 400th incorporated city. The new city then consisted of two country clubs, two hotels, one polo club, a small store and a gas station with two pumps. It was a humble beginning for a small desert city that today has evolved into a one of the most prestigious communities in the Coachella Valley, and one of the most exclusive.

Today, Indian Wells boasts recreational and hotel facilities that draw visitors from around the world - the Hyatt Grand Champions, Renaissance Esmeralda, Desert Horizons Country Club, Indian Wells Golf Resort and many others. Indian Wells is also the home of those who treasure privacy in such exclusive enclaves as The Vintage Club, a paradise within a paradise. And for first class tennis, there is no finer facility in the Coachella Valley than the Indian Wells Tennis Garden, home to world competition.

One can't help but notice the change of ambience when driving along Hwy 111 through Indian Wells. The highway is flanked by impeccably manicured landscaping, serpentine sidewalks and gracefully walled residential communities. Highway 111, as it passes through Indian Wells, is a far cry from the usual patchwork of strip malls, auto dealers and business offices found in other communities. There is a sense of order and beauty that marks Indian Wells as a special neighbor in the Coachella Valley.

Stately Renaissance Esmeralda Hotel, Indian Wells

Palm Desert

XVIII

Palm Desert
Incorporated 1973

The City of Palm Desert is in an ideal location. From the northern portion of the community, the flat desert floor crosses Highway 111 where it slowly rises to the south into the Santa Rosa Mountains. The southern portion of Palm Desert is actually a large alluvial fan that is protected from the winds while offering extra special scenic views of the entire valley. This is "Sand Hole," as it was first called in the early 1930's.

(Courtesy - Historical Society of Palm Desert)
Aerial of upper cove in Palm Desert. All growth was north of Hwy 111

(Courtesy - Historical Society of Palm Desert)
Harvesting onions in Palm Desert

Agriculture began to dominate the landscape with citrus orchards, grape vines and mixed farm crops, including date groves that evolved into a lasting icon for the Coachella Valley.

In 1932, the Palms to Pines highway, officially known as Highway 74, opened carrying vehicles up and over the Santa Rosa Mountains connecting the Coachella Valley with Idyllwild and the San Diego region.

(Courtesy - Historical Society of Palm Desert)
Hwy 111 crossing Palm Desert cove on the left

(Courtesy - Historical Society of Palm Desert)
First home established in the Palm Desert area

Sand Hole was actually not much more than open desert during WWII. By war's end, however, the village was a neighborly community of six houses clustered along Highway 111. Traveling to Palm Springs or Indio along Highway 111 was easy for there was not one traffic signal to slow you down - a far cry from today.

Sand Hole was often called Palm Village in the early days. It served as a tank and truck depot for General Patton's training facility at Camp Young, east of Indio. The vehicle compound was located in the open desert near the intersection of Portola and Highway 111.

(Courtesy - Historical Society of Palm Desert)
Military tanks in the Palm Desert motor pool near Hwy 111 and Portola

(Courtesy - Historical Society of Palm Desert)
Aerial of street layout in Palm Desert. El Paseo Drive in the center picture

After the war, early pioneer Cliff Henderson was so impressed with the natural beauty of the area, its majestic mountain backdrops, palm groves and perfect weather, that he hired engineers to dig for a water source for his *"dream in the making,"* the Shadow Mountain Resort. In 1948, at 600 feet below the surface of the desert, his dream was about to become true. He and a handful of investors discovered water and they knew that they had struck liquid gold. Construction soon got underway. Built as the first destination resort for vacationers coming to the desert, the Shadow Mountain Resort's major feature was the largest swimming pool in the Coachella Valley in the 50s.

In the beginning, all development was north of Highway 111. The two lane highway separated the mountain-side of the valley from the flat, open desert. The City of Palm Desert in central Coachella Valley stimulated all of the communities in the valley to grow, especially along the base and into the coves of the Santa Rosa Mountains.

(Courtesy - Historical Society of Palm Desert)
Beginning construction of the Shadow Mountain Resort - 1950s

(Courtesy - Historical Society of Palm Desert)
Finished Shadow Mountain Resort, the Coachella Valleys' first resort

The Shadow Mountain Resort opened in 1946 with plenty of razzle-dazzle, hula girls on surfboards and tennis greats. It touted its own man made lake, clubhouse and the giant, figure eight swimming pool. The resort was an immediate success and many Hollywood celebrities joined in the activities. A golf course was later added to the facilities.

(Courtesy - Historical Society of Palm Desert)
Opening day celebration at the Shadow Mountain Resort pool

Shadow Mountain Resort today

149

What followed in Palm Desert was the establishment of many country clubs and golf courses - Palm Desert Country Club, Marrakesh, Avondale and Ironwood. Palm Desert today boasts some of the finest resorts and private communities in all of the Coachella Valley - Big Horn, Desert Willow, Marriott Desert Springs, Monterey Country Club, Chaparral, Desert Falls, Palm Valley, Sun City, The Reserve, and many, many others.

World famous El Paseo Drive shopping area

El Paseo Drive, virtually without a single building in the early fifties, has evolved into one of the finest retail shopping areas in Southern California, rivaling the finest shops in chic Beverly Hills. Town centers and malls throughout Palm Desert followed, establishing Palm Desert as a center for retail merchandising in the Coachella Valley.

The Living Desert, Palm Desert's premier desert attraction, is the world renown ecological garden and zoo displaying plants and animals not only native to the Coachella Valley but to nearly every desert in the world. Started in the 1970's on a two hundred acre plot of land, the Living Desert has grown to more than 1,300 acres. It serves as a center of interest for foreign visitors, valley residents and to tens of thousands of school children from the surrounding area.

Scenes from the popular Living Desert

Aerial of The Living Desert acreage prior to construction

As the community grew, it became home to Coachella Valley's first higher education facility, the College of the Desert, a two-year community college. In partnership with COD, the valley's first four-year university, California State University San Bernardino, is now open to the public, and growing. Recognition and enrollment at these educational facilities is not only due to population expansion and need but to high educational standards.
Every weekend throughout the year the campus is the site of the popular and well attended COD Street Fair, where artisans display their creations. A stroll through the displays are not only fun, but rewarding, too.

(Courtesy - Historical Society of Palm Desert)
Wandering desert miner crossing the empty Palm Desert lands

Sand Hole, Palm Village and the Army Tank and Truck Depot site from WWII have grown into the City of Palm Desert. In little more than a half a century these desert sands evolved into one of the most dynamic communities in the Coachella Valley, and its future is just beginning.

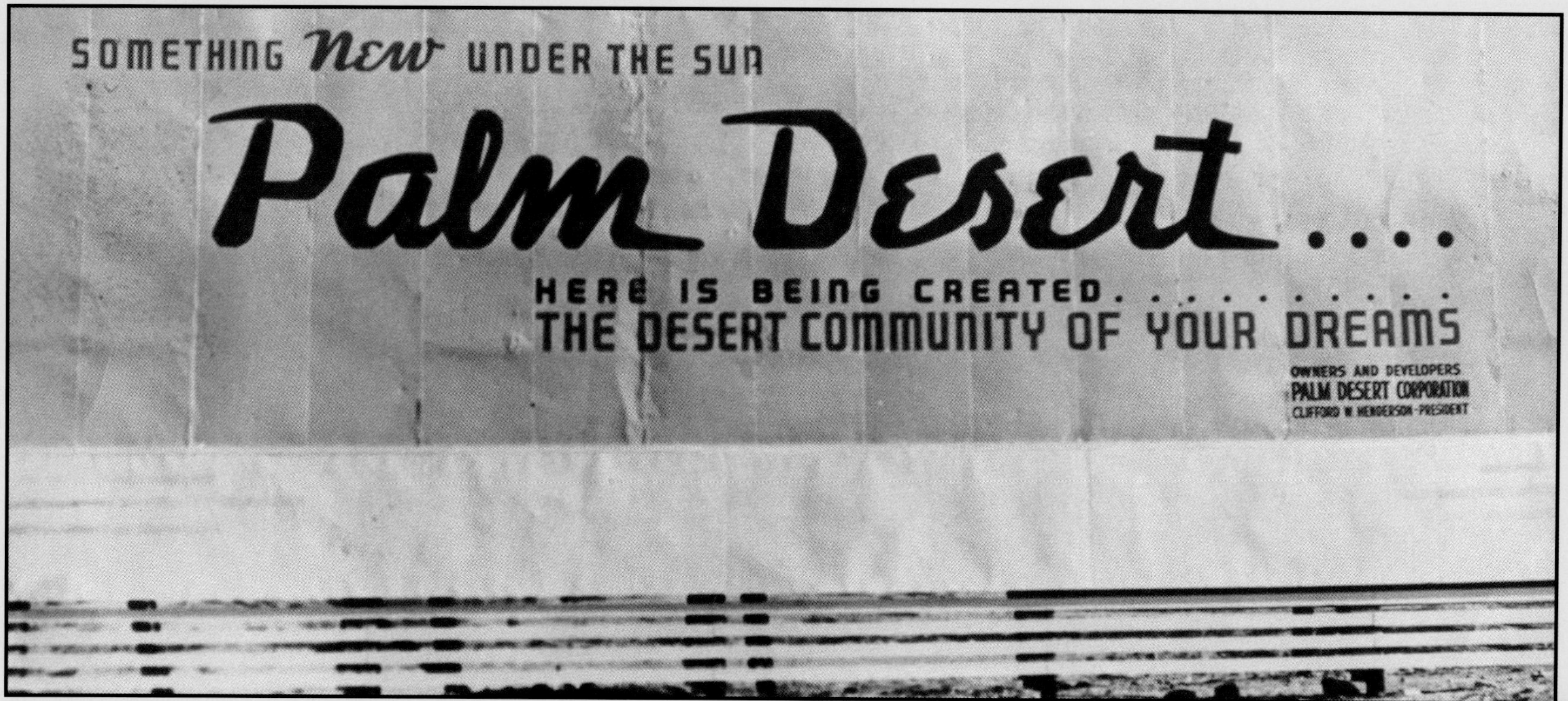

(Courtesy - Historical Society of Palm Desert)
Early billboard designed to attract residents to the Palm Desert area

155

Rancho Mirage

XIX

City of Rancho Mirage
Incorporated 1973

Gold prospectors traveling to the banks of the Colorado River near La Paz, Arizona hopped aboard the Bradshaw Stage Line that crawled through the Coachella Valley desert along the dry belly of the Whitewater River bed. As news of the gold rush spread, the area flourished. The rickety wheels of the Bradshaw Stage were replaced by the Southern Pacific Railroad on the newly laid tracks crossing the desert to Yuma, Arizona and beyond. The rutted wagon trail was completely plowed over and graded. It was named the Bradshaw Highway, the forerunner for today's Highway 111.

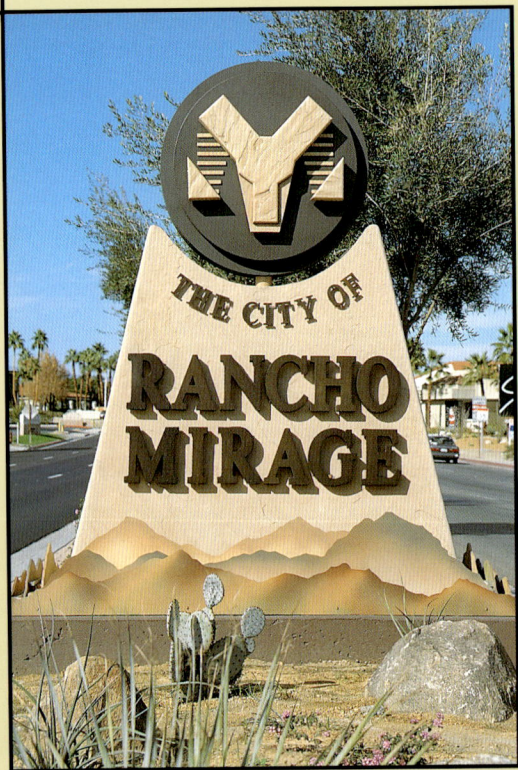

The City of Rancho Mirage site is in a particularly unique location. The land is nestled serenely on the desert floor close to the river bed and is protected from the harsh desert winds by the surrounding Santa Rosa Mountains. Tucked away in a small cove in the Santa Rosas lay pristine Magnesia Falls Canyon, a favorite site of the Cahuilla Indians.

Early developer, Bert Davie, using pioneering ingenuity, gouged out a road through a deep gully using only mules and handmade grading tools. He named the road, *"Rio del Sol,"* road to the sun, and started selling lots in the Rancho del Sol Estates.

(Courtesy - Historical Society of Palm Desert)
Aerial of Rancho Mirage at the end of WWII

Arriving from Santa Monica, California were L.M. Clancy and his wife Helen, who built an adobe home made of bricks from the mud gathered from a nearby wash. Because so many purchasers at Rio del Sol hailed from Santa Monica, the area acquired the nickname, *"Little Santa Monica."* The name of the neighborhood was subsequently changed to Clancy Lane.

Some 300 acres adjacent to Rio del Sol later became the site for the world famous Eisenhower Medical Center, serving the medical needs of the entire Coachella Valley. Through more than a quarter century, the medical facility's reputation has gained worldwide recognition.

(Courtesy - Historical Society of Palm Desert)
Aerial of the land that was destined to become the site of the Eisenhower Medical Center

(Courtesy - Historical Society of Palm Desert)
Early construction of the Eisenhower Medical Center - 1960s

(Courtesy - Historical Society of Palm Desert)
Polo field adjacent to the Mirage Park Airport

(Courtesy - Historical Society of Palm Desert)
Mirage Park Airport and the Desert Air Hotel - 1950s

After the war, Hank Gogetry, fulfilling a long held dream, opened Mirage Park Airport and the Desert Air Hotel, the valley's first fly-in hotel. The facility soon became established as the social center and heart of the community with the hosting of gala parties. Many visitors flew their private planes to the Desert Air Hotel for a weekend jaunt or for a meal at the airport restaurant, just a few feet from where the planes were parked. The Marriott Las Palmas Hotel and Resort and Rancho Las Palmas Country Club now occupy the old airport property.

(Courtesy - Historical Society of Palm Desert)
Mirage Park Airport, presently the site of the Las Palmas Country Club and the Marriott Las Palmas Hotel and Resort

(Courtesy - Historical Society of Palm Desert)
Thunderbird Ranch in the beginning

(Courtesy - Historical Society of Palm Desert)
Aerial of the Thunderbird Ranch in the beginning

The Thunderbird Ranch, a dude ranch operation, was developed in the mid-40's and soon started selling adjacent lots. Ex-mayor of Palm Springs, Frank Bogart, was the Thunderbird Dude Ranch manager in those beginning days. Sensing the growth potential, especially the interest in golf, the dude ranch soon became Thunderbird Country Club with its own 18 hole golf course. Today, there is one golf course in Rancho Mirage for every 1.3 square miles of land.

Lively social parties at Thunderbird were legendary and visited by such celebrities as Edgar Bergan, Ray Bolger, Hoagy Carmichael, Perry Como, Clark Gable, Randolph Scott and Esther Williams, among many others.

Alice Faye and Phil Harris (Courtesy - City of Rancho MIrage)

Lucille Ball and Desi Arnez (Courtesy - City of Rancho MIrage)

Visitors continue to come to Rancho Mirage from all parts of the valley to what has become known as *"restaurant row,"* to visit some of the valley's finest eating establishments that stretch out along Highway 111. The newest addition is The River development complex, a new focal center for dining and entertainment in a city known for fine restaurants. There are so many eateries here that it averages one restaurant for every 200 permanent residents.

More country clubs followed, earning Rancho Mirage the title of *"country club city."* After Thunderbird came Tamarisk, Desert Island, The Springs, Sunrise, Mission Hills, Rancho Las Palmas, Rancho Mirage, Morningside and many others. The allure and prestige of Rancho Mirage Country Clubs continues to draw dignitaries, luminaries and celebrities from around the world.

There have been so many American presidents either living or visiting Rancho Mirage that the community has been called *"the playground of Presidents."*

Giant Saguaros at entrance of the Thunderbird Country Club

Westin Mission Hills Resort & Club entrance

Agua Caliente Casino at I-10 and Bob Hope Drive

Cathedral City

XX

Cathedral City
Incorporated 1981

In 1774, Captain Juan Bautista de Anza led an army of Spanish soldiers surveying the territory from Tubac, Sonora in Mexico to Monterey, California. It was a vast, open land then, and exploring the new lands was vital for Spain to begin to settle the territory. On that trip and others that followed, de Anza stopped in the Coachella Valley, traveling from water hole to water hole along the base of the Santa Rosa Mountains on the land that now encompasses Cathedral City.

In 1850, Col. Henry Washington of the U.S. Army Corp of Engineers explored the area canyons below the Santa Rosas. He was impressed with the architecture of the mountains believing they resembled the interior of a grand cathedral. A survey map created in 1904 identified this area by indicating they contained celestial canyons. The first developers in the area sub-divided the small acreages into plots known as Date Land Ranchos. These first residential developers were so impressed with the mountains that they renamed that first subdivision, Cathedral Canyon, a name that has been identified with the city ever since.

(Courtesy - Historical Society of Palm Desert)
Aerial of Cathedral City - 1950

(Courtesy - Historical Society of Palm Desert)
Two lane Hwy 111 as it passes through Cathedral City - 1930s

Positioned between Palm Springs to the west and Rancho Mirage to the east, Cathedral City lands extend from the Santa Rosas across the Whitewater River and the Interstate. Although most of the land in Cathedral City is held in private ownership, approximately twenty-eight percent of the land is owned by the Agua Caliente Tribe of Cahuilla Indians.

(Courtesy - Historical Society of Palm Desert)
Aerial Cathedral City - 1940s

(Courtesy - Historical Society of Palm Desert)
Blow sand engulf Cathedral City homes

Cathedral City lands extend across what is known as the *"blow sand area."* Even though the wind still blows, it has not restricted the enterprising growth of the city. Golf club resorts and country clubs with their extensive land holdings and landscaping designs are helping tame the blow-sand problem of the past. As new homes are built and landscaped, they too help subdue what was at one time a major problem.

(Courtesy - Cathedral City Historical Society)
View of early Cathedral City from atop the Santa Rosa Mountains. Palm Springs in the distant background

Initially identified as East Palm Springs and later, Palm Springs Heights, Cathedral City and its sordid past was the tempestuous playground of Palm Springs. The most notorious of the hangouts was *"The 139 Club."* The club was not open to Cathedral City residents but only visitors from the Palm Springs area. It was wild and wide open. The city's questionable reputation earned it the name of Cat City - but that was long ago. Today Cathedral City is one of the most diverse communities in the Coachella Valley, with a balanced mix of homes, businesses, country clubs and resort complexes. Cathedral City is growing into a diverse family oriented community.

(Courtesy - Historical Society of Palm Desert)
Early Cathedral City in the 1930s

(Courtesy - Cathedral City Historical Society)
Built in the 1920's, these stone pedestals marked the entrance to Cathedral City. They were torn down in the 1940's to widen Hwy 111

The old *"Gateway to Cathedral City"* arch that identified the city was built in the early 1920's but was torn down in the mid-1940's. The move was necessary to make room for a widening of Hwy 111 from two lanes to a fully paved, four lane thoroughfare. Highway 111 from Indio to Palm Springs at the time was only a two lane road, except for the four lanes that passed through Cathedral City.

In the early 1990's, efforts to create a *"new Cathedral City"* got under way. Old downtown was razed, again making room for another Highway 111 expansion. A new city hall, bell tower and adjacent entertainment structures have been built. Cathedral City is beginning to take its place among Coachella Valley communities as a city rebuilding itself. Cathedral City boasts of its new library near the new High School and Sports Park, creating an infrastructure for a dynamic family oriented community.

The city today is experiencing population growth that is expanding its residential and business development. The remainder of the new city center and rebuilding of the downtown area will take up most of the first decade of the new millennium, assuring that Cathedral City can rightly take its place as a major contributor to the life and vibrancy of the Coachella Valley. Civic leaders and the community are dedicated to building *"the Cathedral City of the Future."*

La Quinta   XXI

La Quinta
Incorporated 1982

According to ancient Cahuilla Indian history, La Quinta was *"the cradle of civilization, where all life on earth began."* If you've ever stood at the top of the La Quinta Cove in a passing storm or watched the clouds billowing over the Santa Rosas, it would be easy to believe that Cahuilla legend. For the many new residents of La Quinta, the fastest growing city in the Coachella Valley, the La Quinta lifestyle is what makes residents firmly believe that residing in La Quinta is the beginning of a special life-experience.

Storm Clouds gather in the Santa Rosa Mountains

Literally rising from beneath the waters of the Gulf of California, as witnessed by the old, ocean water line of the Gulf of California, La Quinta has emerged as one of the fastest growing community in California.

The mountains surrounding the cove are awe-inspiring, one of the most inspirational locations on earth. Matter of fact, high in the La Quinta cove, up above the homes, was the site chosen for the biblical film where Charleston Heston stood on the rock staircase and reached to the sky to touch heaven. Once you experience nature splashing her vivid hues against the rocks, especially at sunrise or sunset, all other mountains seem lackluster by comparison. There's mystery and magic in the mountains of La Quinta creating a feeling that spills over into every day life.

A woman and her dog walk along the banks of the Coachella Canal bringing perspective to the ancient sea water line at the base of the Santa Rosa Mountains

Early Native Americans fished here in a most unusual manner - fish traps. Creating a small rock basin along the edge of the ancient sea, fish would be herded into the traps and held there until dinner time. This long forgotten and dried up edge of the sea is fast becoming the center of living and recreation throughout the entire Coachella Valley.

When gold was discovered in Arizona in 1862, Major William Bradshaw discovered the first trail through the Coachella Valley when he transported gold seekers across the Colorado Desert. Point Happy, at the corner of Washington Street and Highway 111, soon became a landmark for the stagecoaches and freight wagons traveling the Bradshaw trail. The Point Happy stop began its tradition as a hospitable *"watering hole"* for desert travelers long before it became a ranching property known as the Point Happy Date Gardens.

(Courtesy - Historical Society of Palm Desert)
Aerial of the intersection of Washington St. and Hwy 111. Point Happy Ranch - left center

La Quinta was first known as Marshall's Cove. John Marshall and his brother-in-law, Albert Green, homesteaded and divided a 320 acre piece of land where Washington Street ends at Avenue 52. Marshall's property was subsequently sold to William S. Rosecrans, a wealthy Los Angeles businessman who had prospered in oil and real estate investments. The Rosecrans House was built in 1920 and is named for a loving cat that is said to have saved the life of Mrs. Rosecrans from a rattlesnake that was about to strike. Hacienda del Gato today is the administrative building at Tradition, one of La Quinta's premier residential developments.

Matriarch of the community is the Hotel La Quinta, built in 1926. Today, the old hotel, and its original 56 rooms, is surrounded by more than 600 rooms, casitas, tennis courts, 24 swimming pools, spas and conference rooms. The city of La Quinta, named for the hotel, is the only city in the country that has taken the name of a landmark hotel from within city boundaries.

(Courtesy - Coachella Valley Water District)
Old La Quinta airstrip near the intersection of Eisenhower and Ave 50 before La Quinta became a city

Many of Hollywood's brightest stars would make their way to La Quinta to escape from the congestion of the big city. Many would wing in on their private planes, landing directly adjacent to the hotel on the airstrip maintained by the hotel. Irving Berlin often showed up during December with his family, chauffeur and private maid. Here, in the quiet surroundings of the La Quinta Hotel, he wrote the words and music to the classic holiday song, White Christmas.

(Courtesy - Coachella Valley Water District)
Terminal reservoir Lake Cahuilla in early 1980s. The land bordering the reservoir is now PGA West

(Courtesy - Coachella Valley Water District)
Aerial of La Quinta Cove in the 1940s

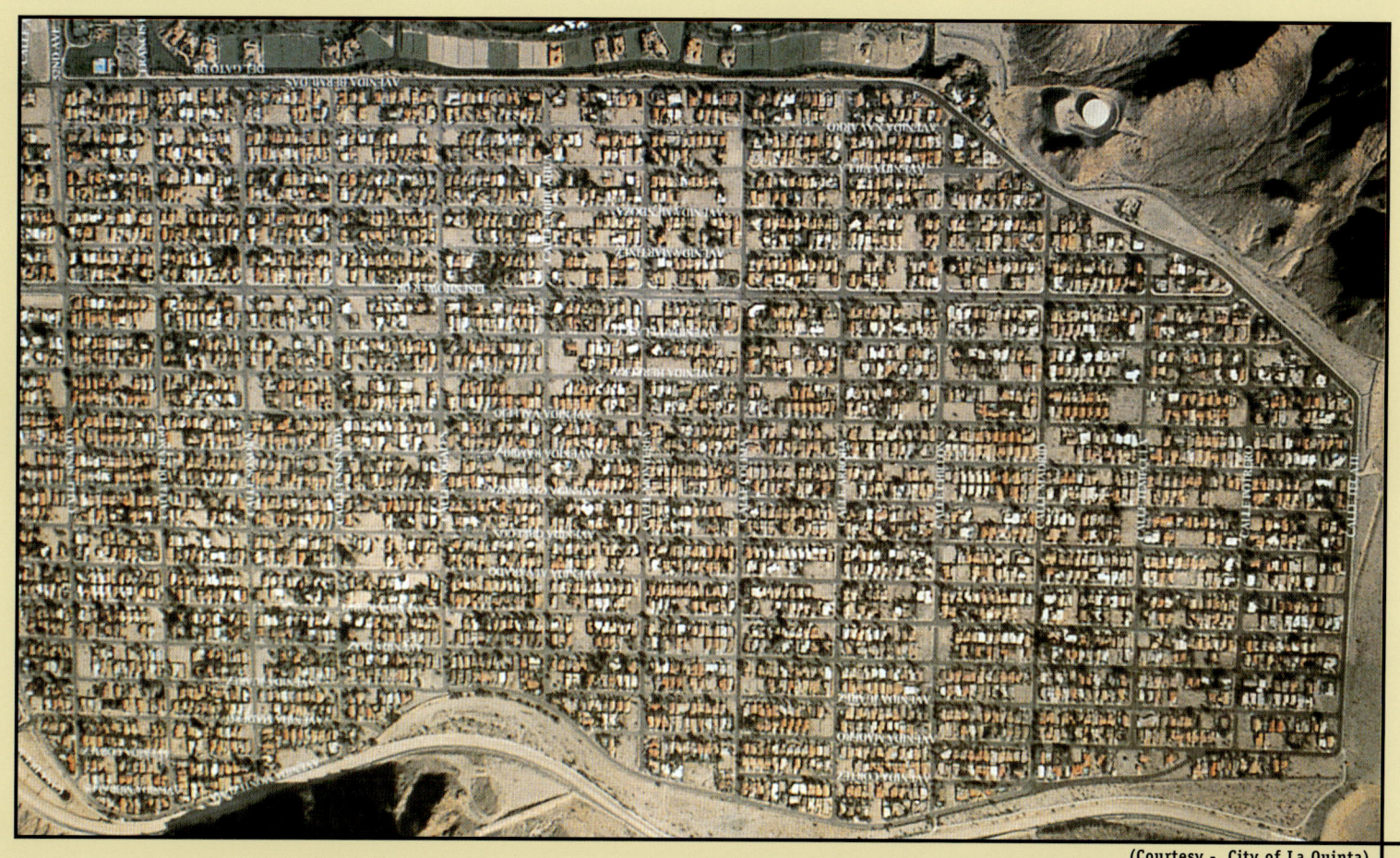

(Courtesy - City of La Quinta)
Aerial of La Quinta Cove homes today

La Quinta has established itself as the art center of the Coachella Valley

New permanent home of the La Quinta Art Festival on Washington Avenue

Magnificent vistas of mountains and luxuriant fairways surround the well-appointed homes of La Quinta

St Francis of Assisi Catholic church on Washington Street

La Quinta today is the fastest growing community in the Coachella Valley and among the top ten communities for growth in California. The potential of La Quinta becoming the largest city in the Coachella Valley is noteworthy for just to the south is open, unincorporated farmland presently under the *"sphere of influence"* by the City of La Quinta.

Coachella Valley's Future

XXII

Coachella Valley's Future

Water and people are what transformed the Coachella Valley from a lifeless, barren desert into one of the most beautiful and desirable areas in which to live, work and play. On the heels of the early farmers and the returning veterans, and for nearly a century, a continuous flow of new people arrived to make the Coachella Valley their home. Initially coming to start a new life in farming, and then to evade the long cold winters, or escape from the stifling congestion of the big cities, many stayed and eventually converted into permanent residents. It's called *"the sand in your shoes syndrome,"* for when one is taken in by the vibrancy and magic of living in the Coachella Valley it's nearly impossible to want to live anywhere else.

Three distinct cultures of the Coachella Valley, Indian, Hispanic and Anglo, have combined to give birth to a blending social order that respects values and traditions, creating an environment conditioned by the beauty of the desert and the valley's sheltered geographic location.

Palm Springs street scene

Colorful flags at the COD Street Fair

At the end of WWII, the Coachella Valley had a population of only a few thousand people, mostly farmers growing crops in the green, eastern end of the valley. Even though vacationers came to the desert during the winter, most businesses closed up shop during the summer - it was just too hot. What turned the Coachella Valley into a major destination resort was the development of air conditioning, opportunity, the expanding recreational amenities such as tennis and golf attracting amateur and professionals alike, and of course, sensational winter weather. Three million vacationers visit this desert every year. Recreation, tourism and agriculture, the driving economic forces in the Coachella Valley are all running full speed.

The popular Palm Springs Air Museum

Horse jumping competition - Indio

Horseback riding near Lake Cahuilla

When today's residents first came to the Coachella Valley, many initially for a visit during the winter months, they found an energetic life style and unsurpassed beauty, unlike any other region in the country. They came for a round of golf or two, perhaps a short weekend jaunt, a family vacation in the spring, or a four-day business conference in the summer. Soon the Coachella Valley started to not only grow, but to grow on you. Although many of today's residents maintain second homes, early residents soon found that the weather, spectacular for nine months of the year, was not as bad during the warmer months as what they had imagined.

Golfing at the Las Palmas Country Club

Tennis at the Shadow Mountain Resort

Clustered mail boxes at Pinion Crest

Arriving at the mountain station - (Courtesy Palm Springs Aerial Tramway)

As visitors quickly became residents, the communities raced to keep pace with the necessities of living - schools, roads, restaurants, golf courses, swimming pools, more restaurants, tennis courts, and more and more homes stretching across the open desert - and more restaurants. And even today, the inflow of new residents moving into the Coachella Valley continues to be as strong today as it has ever been.

For more than a century, migration into the Coachella Valley has not abated. With a population of some 300,000 people at the beginning of the new millennium, it is estimated that by the year 2020, the Coachella Valley will more than double its population to between six and seven hundred thousand people, perhaps more. With approximately 50 new residents moving into the valley every day of the year, it will not be long before the Coachella Valley reaches or exceeds that estimation.

Palm Springs International Airport

Riverside County Annual Date Festival

They all come here to benefit from the outstanding weather, to breathe the clean dry air, to golf, tennis and to swim, to view the clear blue skies, to revitalize mind and body and to live a life style that's envied around the world. Many become permanent residents and wonder why it took them so long to make the decision.

Courtesy Palm Springs Follies
Palm Springs Follies' "long legged lovelies", all in their 50's, 60's, 70's and even their 80's

Desert sky from high in the La Quinta Cove

And the people still come, from every part of the United States and from all over the world. If you're a winter visitor, just look for the out-of-state auto license plates that crowd Highway 111. You can see cars from nearly every state in the United States, as well as from Canada and Alaska. Oregonians and Washingtonians come to escape the rain of the Northwest while those from Minnesota or Wisconsin are freed from the freezing winters of the Midwest.

When you're in the Coachella Valley you're freed from the turmoil of city life, from the high-rise forests and crowded and smoggy freeway congestion of modern cities, from a past that binds and restricts. Over-populated America has discovered the Coachella Valley's pleasurable, enchanting and alluring life style. Somewhat isolated from the rest of the world by towering mountains and expanses of open desert, the Coachella Valley is the focal center of a very special world.

Sunset over the Santa Rosa Mountains

Hot air ballooning at sunset - La Quinta

This is the Coachella Valley of Yesterday, Today and Tomorrow.

Location, geography and climate: The Coachella Valley is about 120 miles south and east of Los Angeles and about 100 miles inland from the coastal city of San Diego. The valley is surrounded on three sides by the San Bernardino, San Jacinto and the Santa Rosa Mountains. Mt. San Jacinto is 10,804 feet in elevation and is covered with snow during the winter. In the San Bernardino Mountains, Mt. San Gorgonio tops out at 11,499 feet. The Santa Rosa Mountains on the south are over 8,000 feet in elevation. The Coachella Valley, about 15 to 20 miles wide and 70 miles long extends from the City of Palm Springs with an elevation of 465 feet until it meets the Salton Sea with a surface of 232 feet below sea level.

The west end of the valley is home to the major population centers of Palm Springs, Desert Hot Springs, Cathedral City, Rancho Mirage, Palm Desert, Indian Wells and La Quinta. The east end, from about Indio and Coachella to the Salton Sea is known as the "green end" of the valley. Here, approximately 80,000 acres are under cultivation growing farm products twelve months of the year.

The climate in the Coachella Valley is quite warm in the summer (105 - 110°) but seldom dropping below the freezing range during winter. During late winter through spring, Snow Bird visitors flock to the valley from around the world to bask in what many consider the most idyllic weather to be found in the country.

Economy: The economy of the Coachella Valley is based on tourism and agriculture. Farm products such as dates, citrus and truck crops are grown and shipped all year long. Employment throughout the valley is heavily oriented to both the tourist service industry and to agriculture. Because of abundant open space, the valley is experiencing dynamic growth and a population influx. Indian gaming is also having a marked influence on the economy.

Population: As of 2004, the population of the Coachella Valley was approximately 350,000 full time residents. During the year an estimated 3,000,000 tourists visit the Coachella Valley. The permanent resident population is growing at about 50 people per day and is expected to double the population in less than twenty years.

ABOUT THE AUTHOR

Richard J. Soltys was born in Los Angeles, California. His interest in photography was always high. He attended the U.S. Navy Photography School in Pensacola, Florida and was assigned to the Pt. Mugu Naval Weapons Missile Test Center where he became involved in photographic activity with early Navy missile programs. Upon graduation from the University of Southern California with a major in Cinema, he worked for two corporate production companies until he started his own company.

The telephone industry kicked off his career working for General Telephone, Pacific Telephone and AT&T. Hawaii called where he produced numerous documentaries for the Hawaiian Sugar Industry and the 100th anniversary documentary for Matson Navigation Company, the company that brought tourism to Hawaii. The Department of Water and Power provided the opportunity to produce a documentary representing the City of Los Angeles at the World's Fair in Osaka, Japan. He maintained an extended relationship with the DWP producing nearly every film or video produced through the department.

His corporate relationships led to producing numerous documentaries throughout the state including: Palm Spring's Desert Water Agency, Palm Springs Historical Society, Coachella Valley Resource Conservation District and the Coachella Valley Water District. His appreciation of history and love of the Coachella Valley helped create this visual interpretation of the past, present and future of the Coachella Valley.

Inside front hard cover - left to right

1. Salt Works train at the Salton Sink - 1904
2. One of the first airplanes to come to the Coachella Valley - 1911
3. Hotel and luncheon rest stop, Oasis area - 1912
4. Thermal Town Hall - 1909
5. Ben Johnson-early date grower - 1904
6. Snow in Palm Springs - 1934

Inside back hard cover - left to right

1. Coachella Post Office and general store - 1909
2. Military tank motor pool - Palm Desert - 1943
3. Model T's in Coachella - 1924
4. Closing the Colorado River break - 1906
5. Gard building - Indio - 1912
6. Women's Club of Indio - 1912